The Way I See It

God, Family, and Other Musings

Margaret Hoskins

Printed and Bound in the United States of America

Professional Publishing House, LLC
1425 W. Manchester Avenue Suite B
Los Angeles, California 90047
323-750-3592
Email: professionalpublishinghouse@yahoo.com
www.Professionalpublishinghouse.com

First printing October 2020
978-1-7328982-4-0
10987654321

All Bible Scriptures are from the King James Version

For inquiries contact:
professionalpublishinghouse@yahoo.com

Acknowledgments

First, I want to thank God for allowing me to live these many years and for the opportunity to pen my story.

I want to thank my sister, Attorney Clara King, for encouraging me to write this book.

Also, my youngest son, Pastor Ricky Hoskins, and his wife, Lalita, for their typing and computer skills they used in helping put this book together.

To my sister, Dr. Rosie Milligan-Bush, I thank you for publishing my book and encouraging me to stay at it. Thank you for keeping us all motivated to push and push until there is no more push in us.

I want to acknowledge my loving children, my firstborn, Ezzard Charles Hoskins, my daughter-in-law, Linda Hoskins, Gloria Hoskins, Rosie Marie Chenault, Shirley Lewis, and son-in-law, Carl Lewis.

I want to acknowledge my sisters: Dr. Rosie Milligan, Owen Nelson, Clara King, Kenyaka

Beckley, Lillie Bell Towns, and Pastor Johnnie Mae Smith; my brothers: Robert Earl Hunter, Leroy Hunter, and his wife, Pearl Hunter; my deceased sisters: Willie Lou Micou and Nellie Bowden, and deceased brother: Willie B Sanders.

Chapter 1

I was born in Como, Mississippi. My precious mother was Florine Hunter. My special father was Simon Hunter. We were a happy family. I was a blessing to have had maternal and paternal grandparents. We all grew up on our grandpa's, John Allen Hunter, farm. We lived about a mile from our paternal grandparents. My great-grandma, Elize Pashcel, lived to be one hundred four years old. She outlived my mother and all seven of her children. When she was ninety years old, she walked a mile to our house for us to wash her clothes on an old rub board. There was no washing machine in those days.

We had to draw water from a well or get water from a pump.

My older sister, who lives in Danville on Elmwood Street, still has a pump in her yard. She waters her flowers from that pump. My grandma, Florence Mitchell, and her mother, Elize, lived to see the electricity in their homes before dying. For many years, all they had were kerosene lamps. I was thirteen years old when we got electricity.

Aunt Bell had a sewing machine she peddled with her feet. She taught my sister, Owen, how to sew on it. Owen learned to sew when she was thirteen and could make any style of clothes and did not use a pattern.

I was thirty-five years old when I learned to sew. I went to tailoring classes at Danville Area Community College for one year. I never thought I would make men's suits, wedding gowns, and bridesmaids dresses. There were women in the community who were good seamstresses, who made their living sewing for people.

My brother, Leroy, worked at General Motors in Los Angeles, California, for thirty years. After he retired, he bought a sewing machine and started sewing, making men's suits, blue jeans, and jackets. Now he has a successful business designing T-shirts, jackets, caps, and selling clothes all over the country.

A lot of us should stir up our gifts. People in the olden days were very creative. Grandma Luevenia would take meat grease and mix it with lye and other things to make soap bars to wash with. Grandma Florence made beautiful quilts, and she did not use sewing machines. She used a needle, thread, and a thimble. When we were teenagers, we always made skirts to wear to church, sewing them with our own hands and not a sewing machine. Aunt Bell had a manual sewing machine she used to turn flour sacks into our underclothes. My sister, Willie, could do beautiful embroidery by hand. Some people didn't have big bank accounts, but they used their brains to survive.

Mom never had a pressure canning, but she used the old black pot for canning all types of fruits. She canned peaches, blackberries, apples, tomatoes, and made jam, jelly, dill pickles, cucumber pickles, and a variety of other jams. Mom kept all the canned fruits in the pantry. It was safer to can fruits than to freeze them.

Daddy was a hardworking man, who went to work on the farm at sunrise and worked for two hours before he would come back home and we all ate our breakfast. He tilled many acres of land to plant his crops. In those days, people did not own a tractor, and plowing up the soil was very hard work. Daddy started putting all his seeds in the soil in March: watermelons, corn, popcorn, peanuts, and white potatoes. We had to put the sweet potato vines in soil with our hands. That was something I did not like to do. Our next work was starting with our garden. I always liked working in a garden and growing a pretty flower garden.

When Daddy told us he was going to build two more rooms onto our house, we thought he was going to have a carpenter to do it. When he started laying the foundation, I asked him, "Where is the carpenter?"

"I am the carpenter," he said to me.

We were astonished. Our house burned down when we were children and Daddy had another house built. We were thinking if he added onto the house it would disfigure the house, but he did a great job.

On the house, he built a nice chimney and fireplace that made us have a nice living room, and Aunt Essie gave us a couch. Men in the country always made benches for the children to sit on, and so did Dad.

Chapter 2

When we were children, we really enjoyed reading books and telling stories. Everyone had their special story, and Dad would read Bible stories with us. He taught us how to live and how to work. The home should be the first place children see good examples as role models for their lives. If they don't see role models of moral character at home, how are they ever going to learn to live responsibly? Parents should not encourage bigotry, prejudice, and narrow-mindedness in the home. Our children need strong home training that show words and examples of Christianity to counteract the selfishness of today.

We should love others and make it plain to them that God is love.

Most children are kindhearted, but some have not had spiritual training in the home. Children learn more from our walk than they do from our talk. Whatever you see in your child, check out your reflection in the mirror. Some parents have trained their children well, but sometimes, they are influenced outside the home. The golden age of childhood is twelve. Childhood maturity, often called the golden age because of the difficult, early teaching years, they have not reached the ever more difficult adolescent growing years, the children focus on events and people outside the home.

Between the ages of thirteen and fifteen, children are generally engaged in major psychological, emotional, and physical changes. They become critical of themselves and others more often than their parents, and they struggle with an awakening of their own identity. They seek to find out who they are and what their role is in life. They relate to people of their own age and are generally more susceptible to influences outside the home.

Some parents may consider there is not enough time to teach children family values; priority is an important consideration here. It is professionalism as possible whether we are office workers, doctors, teachers, or homemakers. Being professional means we make sure we have full knowledge of what we need to do to the best of our ability. We must be professional in our role as parents.

Being a parent is not something we do in the time we have left from our proper jobs. It should be the most important role in our lives. To bring up our children to be wonderful human beings, who will be happy here on earth and happy forever in heaven. Then, we can show others how to live as children of God. There is no greater profession than this privileged task entrusted to us by God.

I believe we were given unique abilities and talents. You are blessed to be a blessing; the true joy of these gifts is only realized when we share them with others. When we were children, Mom and Dad taught us how to help the older people in the neighborhood. We were glad to help our grandparents and senior citizens.

Sex education should be taught in the home, fathers should teach their sons, and mothers their daughters how to keep thyself pure and be examples in purity. Let them know their body is the temple of the Holy Ghost.

Daddy taught his sons how to buy nice clothes and how to dress. Our mother taught us how to dress; she always taught us how to dress appropriately whether for church or a picnic. Also, Daddy would not let us dress any kind of way. But for many people, these virtues are old fashioned. Patriotism is out and civil disobedience is in and the new morality is in and self-discipline is out. I see girls going to school wearing short tops and boys with their pants down their behinds. I was talking to their parents about the way they were dressing, and the parents said that they go to work before their children go to school.

If parents would teach their children how to dress it would not make a difference if they left home early or not. Our parents did not stand around to see how we were dressed; we knew how to because they taught us how.

1. *Children should be taught to remember thy Creator in the days of thy youth.* Ecclesiastes 12:1

2. *Children should be taught to fear God.* Proverbs 24:21

3. *Children should be taught to obey God.* Deuteronomy 30:2

4. *Children should be taught to honor their parents.* Exodus 20:12

5. *Children should be instructed in the way of the Lord.* Deuteronomy 31:12

6. *Children should be taught the way of salvation.*

John 3:16

7. *Foolishness is bound in the heart of a child, but the rod of correction shall drive it far from them.* Proverbs 22:26

8. *A child left to himself bringeth his mother to shame*. Proverbs 29:15

Respect for God and His people must be taught, and we must teach respect for the church. This begins with early training of attitude to the building itself. From infancy, children should be sensitive to the church as a special honored place and taught that the sanctuary has sacred importance. Daddy was a Sunday School teacher for many years, also a deacon and church secretary.

Chapter 3

Daddy taught his children basic financial responsibilities. We had a good foundation for teaching Christian Stewardship and tithing, how to make the first allowance of ten pennies. Then the concept of tithing can be understood by even a very young child: one penny out of every ten is the Lord's. When children are older, they will understand the extra giving above tithes. Daddy gave all of us money to put into church. I gave one of our church members a ride to church for fifteen years. She told me she did not make enough money to give tithes to the church because she worked at a nursing home. I explained to her it does not matter how much money you make, just give ten percent of that.

We always said our prayers every night before we went to bed. "Now I lay me down to sleep, I pray the Lord my soul to keep. If I should die before I wake, I pray the Lord my soul to take." This was always the children's prayer. By the age of eight years old, we could recite the Lord's Prayer in unison. By the teenage years, we learned how to pray our own prayers, because prayer is the simplest words of the mouth and the earnest desire of the heart.

I remember when Daddy was sick. My little great-granddaughter, Niesha, would come over and pray for Daddy. She was praying out of her heart for God to heal her great-grandpa. A prayer model can lead children through the key elements of prayer so they can communicate with God. Honor God's name, our Father; God is your heavenly hallowed be your name, which means "may your name be honored." Matthew 6:9 Jesus says to pray, *your kingdom come, your will be done on earth as it in in heaven.* When children pray these words, they are learning to yield to God's will and plans. When the disciples implored, *Lord teach us how to pray*, Luke 11:1, Jesus responded by providing a prayer model for His followers found in Luke 11:1-2.

James 5:13 states, *is any among you afflicted? Let him pray. Is any merry? Let him sing psalms.*

James 5:16 states, *Confess your faults one to another and pray one for another that you may be healed. The effectual fervent prayer of the righteous man availeth much.*

John 15:7 says, *If you abide in me and my words abide in you, ye shall ask what you will, and it shall be done unto you.*

2 Peter 3:9 says, *the Lord is not willing that any should perish.*

We are to pray for those outside the body of Christ, but we must not forget that the person for whom we are praying has free will just as you and I have. It is God's will that we pray that everyone will be saved in answer to our prayers.

Are we asking amiss? James writes, *Ye ask and receive not because ye ask amiss, that you may consume it upon your lusts.* 1 John 5:14-15 states, *and this is the confidence that we have in Him, that if we ask anything according to His will, He hearth us and if we know that He hears us, whatsoever we ask, we know that we have the petitions that we desired of Him,* how can we have confidence in anything we ask? It is by praying according to His will, *"The Lord is not willing that any should perish."*

With the older people, every time the plan to do something would go array, they would always say it be the Lord's will. When we pray in that way, we are praying the perfect will of God. The spirit knows the mind of God and helps us when we don't know how to pray as we ought, which is all too often. Have you ever been glad that God did not answer some of your prayers? Or that He didn't answer them the way you intended when you prayed?

Matthew 6:6 states, *"But thou, when thou prayest, enter into thy closet, and when thou hast shut thy door, pray to thy Father which is in secret; and thy Father which seeth in secret shall reward thee openly."* Let us pray that our grandchildren will live faithful lives and receive God's blessings.

Proverbs 28:2 says, *even the small everyday habits of life are important and can bring glory to God.* Paul put it like this: *"So whether you eat or drink or whatever you do, do it all for the glory of God."* We tend to overlook the importance of being faithful in the small things of life. If you would mow the lawn for the elderly, that is as great as you operating an airplane.

Colossians 3:23 says, *"And whatsoever ye do, do* it *heartily, as to the Lord, and not unto men."* If we teach our grandchildren, they will have a growing desire to understand and do God's will. Romans 12:2 says, *"And be not conformed to this world: but be ye transformed by the renewing of your mind, that ye may prove what is that good, and acceptable, and perfect, will of God."* Our grandchildren acknowledge God in all their decisions and choices and allow Him to direct their paths.

Proverbs 3:5-6 says, *[5]Trust in the Lord with all thine heart; and lean not unto thine own understanding. [6]In all thy ways acknowledge Him, and He shall direct thy paths."*

Proverbs 20:11 says, *"Even a child is known by his doings, whether his work be pure and whether it be right."*

The best things you can do for your children and grandchildren is to lead them to God and teach them the word of God.

The second-best thing is to teach them how to read. The thing is to teach them to think for themselves and to develop self-confidence. These things are the prescriptions for a healthy life. They will need these to weather the storms of life and to fight life's battles.

Your children need to know and have a relationship with God because God is their protector. He is the one whom they can always lean and depend upon. He is the same, His love is unconditional.

Chapter 4

I am sure every parent has a Bible in their home. I had a Bible study in my home with fifteen children ages ten to fifteen. I asked them what was the first book in the Bible, didn't one of them know. They all go to church every Sunday; however, I know they do not sit down and study the Bible as adults do. They should remember the first book in the Bible, Daddy used to say, "You need to know how to read for yourself because folks will tell you anything."

Grandmothers can change the dismal illiteracy plight for these children. Women rearing children alone need much help. Many single women are very frustrated having to be the breadwinner for the family. Many must work two jobs or work plus go to school in hopes of improving their financial condition. These women are tired when they come home and do not have the time or stamina to help their children learn to read. This is a time when grandmothers are needed to assist.

Many grandmothers are rearing their grandchildren, needing to step up to the plate to teach their grandchildren to read and write and proper manners.

Manners in the olden days meant saying:

- "Thank you,"
- "Yes, Ma'am,"
- "Please," and
- Addressing grown folks as Mr. and Mrs.

Children were taught to bless their food, say their prayers before going to bed, respect and obey adults and do unto others as you want them to do unto you.

Chapter 5

My sister, Dr. Rosie Milligan, in Los Angeles, California, which is the owner of Professional Publishing House, donated me one hundred books. I have started a book reading club at my home. Dr. Milligan has sponsored Black Writers on Tour for twenty-five years.

Last year, I sponsored my first Black Writers on Tour in Danville. I was surprised at how many people had written books in Danville. We had people to travel from across the country. All races were a part of the Black Writers on Tour, but in Danville, some of my white friends asked if they could come. Next time, I may change the title to All Writers on Tour so everyone will feel free to come.

Working with children has always been a part of my life. I have started a book reading club at my home every Saturday. I also teach them spiritual songs. We try to get these young people involved in different activities. Maybe they will have a better attitude about life. Too many of our teenagers are giving birth to babies at the age of fifteen or sixteen years old, and their mothers and grandparents must take care of and raise these children. The young men want to be a daddy when they cannot buy one pair of shoes for a baby.

Chapter 6

My mother died when I was seventeen years old, My sister became the mother of the household. I thank God we had a Christian daddy. After two years, Daddy remarried to a lady named Zulena, and she was a good stepmother. My cousin, Lou Dora, from Saint Louis, Missouri came down for me and I went home with her. She got me a job at the restaurant where she worked. That was where I met James Hoskins.

We dated for a year before James bought me an engagement ring. I did not like living in Saint Louis so I moved to Memphis when my sister, Willie Lou.

After James saw that I was not coming back, he came on the Memphis train and that was where we got married. We made our home in Memphis. After we separated, my brothers wanted me to come to Los Angeles to live, but Daddy did not want me to go that far from home. He thought it was too far for me and the children to get back home.

I came to Danville for a visit, got a job, and stayed on in Danville. I went around in the neighborhood, trying to find a baby sitter. Most everyone told me they did not babysit. I knocked on a woman's door by the name of Ruth Jones. I did not know her and she said, "Yes." After she found out what my salary was and my being a single parent, she babysat for no pay. She was a Christian woman. Many times, when I got home from work, she had already given my children dinner. That is what you call a great missionary.

Ruth had three children herself. Her husband, J.B., worked at General Motors, and he was like a brother to us.

Chapter 7

When I first came to Danville in 1960, there were very nice caring people in the neighborhood. When new people would move into the neighborhood, the other neighbors would always go over and welcome them to the area. People do not do that anymore.

When we lived in the Carver Park complex, we all were like one big family. Children always had respect for the elderly. I always kept my children busy and on Sundays, we went to Sunday School at 10:00 a.m., followed by church service at 11:00 a.m., then at 3:00 p.m., we were back at church and then meet again at 6:00 p.m., for Christian Education.

I also organized a children's choir in the community. Their name was The Wings of Glory and we would sing at different churches.

I was a 4-H Leader for many years and taught baking classes for teenagers and young adults. When my daughters were teenagers, they loved to cook.

My oldest son, Charles, always told me when he graduated from high school, he was going to get a job and buy me a house. He got a job at Cheesecake Factory. He put one hundred dollars in the bank every week until he saved enough money to make a down payment on a house for me. He was not married at the time but wanted to make sure I had a house. After he got married years later, he bought him and his family a house.

When all my children were in high school, they worked part-time jobs. In 1978 there were jobs provided for kids during the summer months for CEDA. When my children were in middle school, there were classes like home economics where kids learned how to sew, cook, crochet, and knit. That was taken out of the schools along with prayer, but it looks like they cannot take out the fighters and gun shooting. Seamstresses are very needed in town; someone always needs sewing done. Jobs had closed in Danville and no unemployment office, and this causes young kids to stand on the street corners and sell drugs and rob other poor people.

Chapter 8

The Bible says money answers all things. Ecclesiastes 10:19, also says, *for the love of money is the root of all evil*, 1 Timothy 6:10. It is all right to have money but the love of money, that is when a person will do any evil thing to get it.

It is right before our eyes; the government has legalized marijuana because they want to tax it and they don't care who it hurts. Whiskey is killing people every day but the whiskey stores still sells it. 2 Timothy 3:1-7 says, *This know also that in the last days perilous times shall come, for men shall be lovers of their selves, covetous, boasters, proud, blasphemers, disobedient to parents, unthankful unholy, without natural affections, trucebreakers, false accusers, incontinent, fierce, despisers of those that are good, traitors, heady, high-minded, lovers of pleasure more than lovers of God.*

In John 16:3, Jesus says, *These things I have spoken unto you, that in me ye might have peace. In the world ye shall have tribulation: but be of good cheer; I have overcome the world.*

We all have our share of trouble and always will, but the presence of trouble does not alter personal responsibility.

James 3:7-8 states, *For every kind of beast, and of birds and of serpents, and of things in the se, it tamed, and hath tamed of mankind, but the tongue can no man tame, it is an unruly evil full of deadly poison.*

James 3:14 says, *But if ye have bitter envying and strife in your hearts, glory not and lie not against the truth.*

James 3:16 says, *For where envying and strife is, there is confusion and every work.*

God is not the author of confusion

Chapter 9

Many have been born again and baptized in the Holy Spirit we do not realize the need for consecration, yet consecration is the only way to the full and victorious Christian life. Consecration then is choosing to walk with Jesus every day. It means putting Jesus first in your life and going His way. *"Seek ye first the Kingdom of God and His righteousness, and all these things shall be added unto you,"* Matthew 6:33

Jesus said *"If any man will come after me, let him deny himself and take up his cross and follow me,"* Luke 9:23

Are willing to go all the way, the songwriter says, I started with Jesus and I've got to go through.

If we are Christ-like, we need the mind like Christ.

1. Philippians 2:2, *Fulfil ye my joy, that ye likeminded, having the same love, being of one accord, of one mind.*
2. Let nothing be done through strife or vainglory, but in lowliness of mind.
3. Let this mind be in you which was also in Christ Jesus.
4. Titus 2:6, Y*oung men likewise exhort to be sober-minded.*

We sing this song in church, "I woke up this morning with my mind stayed on Jesus." I hear people say I got to make up my mind, some people say my mind is made up. If Christ lives in us, He controls our minds, and our lives, we begin to think like He thinks and love like he loves. We then are capable of loving our neighbor as ourselves. When we begin to love as Jesus loves, we begin to desire new life for others as Christ does, *truly I say to you as you did it to one of the least of these my brethren you did it to me,* Matthew 25:40.

1 John 4:11: *Beloved, if God so loved us, we also ought to love one another, no man hath seen God at any time, if we love one another God dwelleth in us, and his love is perfected in us.*

Matthew 5:43, *Jesus said ye have heard that it hath been said, thou shalt love thy neighbor, and hate thine enemy, But I say unto you, love your enemies, bless them that curse you, do good to them that hate you, and pray for them which despitefully use you and persecute you.*

Chapter 10

We can see today that people in the church hate people because of their race. 1 John 3-15 says, *whosoever hated his brethren is a murderer, and ye know that no murderer hath eternal life abiding in him.*

I heard a lady on Fox News Channel say that "People hate President Trump and Trump ought to hate them back" and that is sad. That lady needs Christ in her life, I hope she does not teach her children to hate people. A baby does not know anything about being prejudice, it is taught by the parents. It would be better if parents would teach their children that

God loves us, and we should show love to all. Even Christian families teach their children to hold grudges and make judgments against those who fall by the wayside.

Many children first hear negative comments about other people right in their homes. If a person is raised in a home where gossip is not allowed, that person will be reluctant to participate in gossip throughout their lives. If anyone in my family ever made the mistake of saying something unkind about someone at my home, Daddy would always stop the conversation. Daddy always told us not to repeat what other people say. He told us when you hear nothing, say nothing, because a lie can spread like a wildfire. This is one of the six things that the Lord hates. Revelations 7:8 says, *all liars shall have their part in the lake which burneth with fire and brimstone, which is the second death.*

Romans 12:14, *Bless them which persecute you, bless and curse not.* Romans 12:21 says, *Be not overcome of evil, but overcome evil with good.*

Colossians 3:25 says, *But he that doeth wrong shall receive for the wrong which he had done, and there is no respect of person.*

Ecclesiastes 12:14 says, *For God shall bring every work into judgment, with every secret thing whether it be good or whether it be evil.*

Romans 8:27 says, *And he the searcheth the heart knoweth what is in the mind.*

God is inescapable, there is no place we can hide from Him. God is omnipresence, being present everywhere. God is omniscient, having total knowledge, knowing everything. God is omnipotent, having power without limit.

Christians will be judged at the judgment seat of Christ, 2 Corinthians 5:11. A test of fidelity to Christ as a practical Christian this judgment of believers will determine their rewards. Reward is the recompense for work done, Revelations 22:12, some will have no work.

There is also judgment for the unbelievers and his work. This is called the great white throne judgment,

Revelations 20:11. It is a throne of eternal justice, it is not a human court.

Jesus Christ is the same yesterday, and today and forever, Hebrews 13.

Ephesians 4:6 says, *one God and father of all who is above all, and through all, and in you all.* Are you serving a different God? When there's only one true God.

Chapter 11

When all born again believers in Christ will come together as one complete unit, building on the foundation of our Savior Jesus Christ. As Christian believers, we are responsible for teaching men and women, according to the Bible, how to fulfill their responsibilities and how to live in this corrupt world.

The poser of one is an awesome force. If Christian leaders of the different denominations would come together in one accord in these evil days, I believe sincerely the Lord would pour out His spirit as He did on the day of Pentecost.

Christians in the early church were called saints in the New Testament. All of the people of God enjoy the title "saint," which simply means "Holy one." To be a saint means to be separated. It also means more than that. The Saint is to be one who is in a vital process of sanctification. We are to be purified daily in the growing pursuit of holiness. If we are justified, we must also be sanctified.

1 Peter 15 reads, *But as he which hat called you in holy, so be ye holy in all manner of conversation, because it is written, be ye holy for I am holy*. Acts 2:38 says, *To become a Christian is to repent.*

To become a Christian is to be converted, Acts 3:19.

To become a Christian is to be forgiven, Psalms 103:11.

To become a Christian is to be born again, John 3:1.

If someone were to ask, "What is a Christian?" the response would be that this is he who has accepted the aim and ideas of Christ as their way of living.

The word Christian occurs only three times in the New Testament and not at all in the Old Testament. The word came from the Greek "Christo" and the suffix "I am" means *an adherent or follower*. To become a Christian one must be born into the family of God and is not something you can join. Jesus plainly stated to Nicodemus, "ye must be born again." Likewise, those who become Christians today must become so in this self-same way, "born" into the family of God through the aid and assistance of the Holy Spirit. Certain processes take place. When one is born into the family and we must look at these processes carefully. Redemption means to buy back or to deliver on from something by a price paid, Galatians 3:13. Regeneration is not the reformation of the old life or a change made in the old fleshly nature. Regeneration is the imparting to the individual a brand-new nature 2 Corinthians 5:17.

Repentance means is melanoma in Greek, and is translated as repentance which simply means *a change of mind*. A sinner, through the Holy Spirit, becomes convinced that he is a sinner and changes his mind and attitude towards God and God's law. This leads him to realize that he needs salvation, which is something he cannot provide for himself. Acts 36:5. Religion is a system of faith

James 1:26, *If any man among you seem to be religious and bridleth not his tongue, but deceived his own heart, this man religion is vain.* Pure religion and undefiled before God and the Father is this, to visit the fatherless and widows in their affection, and to keep himself unspotted from the world. Psalms 34:13, *Keep the tongue from evil and thy lips from speaking guile.*

<u>Salvation</u> in the New Testament is deliverance from sin and eternal punishment brought through death and resurrection of Christ, Romans 6:10, and Luke 2:11.

Crossing the Red Sea was called a salvation, Exodus 14:13. Saved, rescued, and delivered from sin, Isaiah 35:4.

Sanctified means made Holy dedicated to sacred use, Hebrew 12:14, follow peace with all men, and holiness without no man hall see God.

Holy is the character and conduct of those who have experienced salvation by which the very life of Christ is being lived out in them.

Sanctification is the state or place where God the Father separated us by the new birth, it is the word of God. 1 Corinthians 1:30.

Sanctification is to be set apart to serve God.

How is such a baptism describe? Therefore, we are buried with him by baptism in the death, that like as Christ was raised from the dead by the glory of the Father even so were shall be also in the likeness of his resurrection.

For if we are planted together in the likeness of His death, we shall be also in the likeness of His resurrection.

Baptism is a gospel ordinance commemorating the death, burial, and resurrection of Christ. In baptism public testimony is given to the effect that the baptized has been crucified with Christ, buried with him, and is raised with him to work the newness of life.

John the Baptist had foretold the baptism, he said, I indeed baptize you with water unto repentance, but He that cometh after me is mightier than I, whose shoes I am not worthy to bear, he shall baptize you with the Holy Ghost and with fire, Matthew 3:11.

The four evangelists: Matthew, Mark, Luke, and John in this place just cited and the apostle Peter. Acts 11:16, if you will read these references carefully and compare them you will see in each case it is not salvation that is spoken of, but a second experience.

This is called in the scripture the baptism in the Holy Spirit because it is a baptism meaning a drenching, overflowing, or saturating of your soul. Jesus causes the spirit to rise and overflow from where He is living inside us. It is important to remember that the Holy Spirit is living in you. He can flood your soul and body.

Jesus says he that believeth on me out of his belly shall flow rivers of living water. (The Holy Ghost) John 7:38. The amplified Bible says "out of his innermost being shall flow".

Chapter 12

What is a church? The church has been regarded as a brotherhood or family. The services were at first in the home of members. Romans 16:3-5, Colossians 4:15, in the Gospels the word appears but twice indicating the fact that the development of the idea institution was not accelerated until some decades after the crucifixion. As the institution continued to grow the dictionary describes it as a building where religious services were held, especially one for Christian worship. A particular group of Christians who have the same beliefs and forms of worship.

Matthew 16:18, *Upon this rock I will build my church, and the gates of hell shall not prevail against it.*

Messages sent by angels to seven churches:

To the church of Ephesus: Revelations 2:1-7

To the church of Thyatira: Revelations 2:18-29

To the church of Sardis: Revelation 3:1-6

To the church of Philadelphia: Revelation 3:7-13

To the church of Smyrna: Revelations 2:8-11

To the church of Pergamum: Revelations 2:12-17

To the church of Laodicea: Revelations 3:14-19

These sevens are in the Bible;

Genesis 21:30 says, *And he said, for these seven owe lambs shalt thou take of my hand, that they may be a witness unto me, that have dug this well.*

Numbers 31:24 seven times

Joshua 6:4 seven priests, seven trumpets

Joshua 18:5 seven parts

Judges 18:5 seven locks

1 Kings 18 seven thousand

2 Kings 4:36 child sneezed seven times, and the child opens his eyes

Revelations 8:6 seven angels, seven trumpets

Revelations 5:6 seven spirits

Revelations 1:20 seven golden candlesticks, seven starts, seven churches

Exodus 22:30, likewise shalt thou do with thine oxen, and with thy sheep, seven days it shall be with his dam; on the eighth-day thou shalt give it me.

Genesis 2:3 God ended his work in seven days

Acts 6:3 Seven men

2 Kings 5:14 dipped himself seven times in Jordan River

God's purpose for this church age:

- What is the divine purpose for this age ending when Jesus returns?

- Acts 15:14, Romans 11:25

- Did Jesus commission believers to convert to the entire world?

- Matthew 24:14
- What is given as one of the comings of the Lords? 1 Thessalonians 5:3
- What is prophesied concerning conditions near the end of this church age?
- 2 Thessalonians 2:3
- Will gospel preaching be popular in the last days? 2 Timothy 4:3-4
- What will increase before Christ come? 2 Peter 21
- Will false teaching prevail? 2 Peter 2:2
- What attitude will many religious leaders take toward the truth of the Lords coming? 2 Peter 3:3-4
- After one has been born of the spirit, what exhortation applies to him?
- Ephesian 5:18, Acts 6:3

- Having received the Spirit through union with Christ, how does on received the fullness of the spirit for service? Romans6:13-16
- How may we have the fullness of power for service? John 7:37-39
- What is the instrument through which men are born of God? James 1:18
- Salvation is offered to the unsaved as a gift, Romans 6:23
- What will Christ do about believer's works when He comes for His own?
- 1 Corinthians 3:11-14, Revelations 22:12
- To win reward what must we do? 1 Corinthians 3:8
- Can anyone labor for salvation? John 6:28-29
- For what will a special crown be given? James 1:12

- On what foundation must these works be built for the believers to receive a crown? 1 Corinthians 3:11-15

- According to scripture will His coming be literal and personal or spiritual such as the progress of knowledge and social justice?
- Acts 1:11, 1 Thessalonians 4:15, Revelations 1:7
- When He comes to reign, how will He be manifested to the world?

- Matthew 24:27

- What did Jesus say about the time of His second coming? Matthew 24:38
- Acts 1:7
- Will the world be converted before His second coming? Matthew 4:38-39

- Since no one knows the time of His coming, what exhortation did Jesus leave for His people? Matthew 24:42, 25:13

- What hint did Jesus give His disciples as to the length of time it might take before He returns? Matthew 25:19

- When He returns in power and glory, what will He do? Matthew 25:31-32

- For when we were yet without strength in due time without strength, in due time Christ died for the ungodly.

- But God commended His love toward us, in that, while we were yet sinners Christ died for us. Roman 5:6-8

- As for me and my house, we will serve the Lord.

- The doom of Satan, what is prepared for the devil? Matthew 25:41

- What will be done to him when Jesus comes? Matthew 20:1-3

- What will take place after the thousand years? Revelations 20:7-9

- What will be Satan's final Doom?

- What will become of all His works? 1 John 3:8

I will not serve Satan and his army.

The Horrors of Hell- Matthew 13:47-50

- The nations who forget God will be there. Psalms 9:17

- The angels who sinned will be there. 2 Peter 2:4

- The devil, the beast, and the false prophets will be there. Revelations 19:10-20

- The ones whose names are not written in the book of life will be there. Matthew 25:41

- Hell will be a place of fire and brimstone. Revelation 19:20

- Hell will be filled with literal fire. Matthew 5:25
- Hell will have fire that never shall be quenched. Mark 9:44
- There will be gnashing of teeth in hell. Matthew 15:42
- There will be thirst that never shall be quench. Luke 16:24-45
- There will be no rest in hell. Revelations 14:11
- There will be a continual torment in hell. Revelations 20:10
- There will be a memory of God's love. John 3:15
- There will be a memory of gospel sermons. Romans 10:17

- There will be memory of invitation to receive Jesus Christ which was rejected. Revelation 22:17
- Hell has been enlarged to hold the multitude that will be there. Isaiah 5:14
- Hell is everlasting in duration. Matthew 25:46

What does anybody want in Hell? This is the works of Satan.

Chapter 13

In this world children are beaten, battered, and kidnapped. Sexually abused by individuals or in their own homes and communities. Since 1974 more than twenty million babies in the United States have died through intentionally aborted pregnancies. Violence attacks our youth every day and over 135,00 kids carry guns and weapons to school and sometimes they open fire and kill innocent classmates. The average age of first-time drug use is thirteen years of age. The god of this world hath blinded the minds of the people.

The thief cometh not but to steal, kill, and destroy but Jesus said I have come to give life and that more abundantly, John 10:10

For the wages of sin is death, but the gift of God is eternal life through Jesus Christ our Lord, Romans 6:23

The tender Jesus will be the judge who sentences people to hell, John 5:22.

Jesus is going to read everybody's verdict and He is going to hand down the sentence. There is a court that is higher than the supreme court. One day we will all stand before the righteous judge.

I admire my children, grandchildren, and my great-grandchildren for graduating from high school and continuing their education, also my nieces and nephews.

This is a list of whose who graduated from a higher level of education.

1. Ricky Hoskins, Bachelor's of Science, Major in General Studies and Minor in Psychology. Eastern Illinois University.

2. Rosie Chenault; Bachelor's in Social Work. Eastern Illinois University

3. Alexis Hoskins; Bachelor's in Criminology/ Sociology, and Black world studied. Dominican University River forest Illinois.

4. Troy Hoskins; Bachelor's in Social Work. Oakwood University. Huntsville Alabama.

5. Myrah Hoskins; Master's in Biology, University of Alabama, Huntsville.

6. Lestan Hoskins; Bachelor's from Judson University, Trinity Evangelic Divinity College, Deerfield Illinois.

7. Jennifer Hoskins; Bachelor's from Southern Illinois University, Master's in Education from Concordia University, Portland Oregon.

8. Starla Lipscomb; Bachelor's in Education, Illinois State University.

9. Ezzard C. Hoskins Jr. Associates in Science, Nassau Community College, New York.

10. Charlene Hoskins; Bachelor's of Science in Biological Science, Hampton University, Master's of Science in Family & Consumers Science Diabetics, Eastern Illinois University.

11. Jessica G. Hoskins; Associates from Parkland Community College, Bachelor's in Education, Illinois State University, Master's in Education, Eastern Illinois University.

12. Donica Wheeler, BSN Bachelor's in Nursing, Lakeview School of Nursing

13. Ervin Wheeler, Bachelor's in Art, Eastern Illinois University

14. Kesha Brown, Bachelor's from Western University, Atlanta Georgia

15. Dr. Terrion L. Williamson, Graduate from the University of Chicago, Bachelor's of Art in English and African American Studies,

University of Illinois College of Law Degree of Juris Doctor, University of Southern California, Master's in American Studies and Ethnicity and Ph.D. (Doctoral) Degree in American Studies and Ethnicity.

16. Tina Nelson-Jackson, Doctorate in Educational Leadership and Management, Capella University, Minneapolis, Minnesota.

17. Sydney D.L. Thomas, Bachelor's of Science, Criminal Justice Homeland Security, Savanna State University.

18. Sabrina D. L. Nelson, Associates of Science Criminal Justice, Macon State College.

19. Denise Derrickson, Bachelor's from Georgia State College, Master's in Social Work, University of Illinois.

20. Aaron Carter, Bachelor's in Business Administration, Clark University Atlanta Georgia

21. Richard Carter, Physician, Emory University Atlanta Georgia.

22. TaKavion Hoskins, Associates Danville Area Community College

23. LaToyia Willis, Surgical Technology, Indiana State University.

24. Tissia Henderson, Fayetteville State University, Master's Mental Health, and Hospital Social Work.

25. Charles Henderson, Bachelor's in Business Management, University of Maryland, Master's in Management, Indian Wesley University.

26. Essence is attending Indiana State University.

27. Eric Smith is attending Normal University, Bloomington, Illinois

28. LaDasia More is attending Indiana State University

29. DaJamil Hoskins is attending Knox College.
30. Tanisha Hoskins, granddaughter, Bachelor's of Science in Nursing, Purdue University Northwest

www.ingramcontent.com/pod-product-compliance
Lightning Source LLC
LaVergne TN
LVHW050943080826
845145LV00004B/1394

* 9 7 8 1 7 3 2 8 9 8 2 4 0 *